The South Shore Phrase Book

THE SOUTH SHORE PHRASE BOOK

Compiled by Lewis J. Poteet

Concordia University

Montreal

The words and phrases collected in this book are from the coastal villages between St. Margaret's Bay, near Halifax, and Woods Harbour, near Yarmouth, the South Shore of Nova Scotia. If no place of origin is given, the item is used more or less throughout the area.

LANCELOT PRESS

Hantsport, Nova Scotia

ISBN 0-88999-192-8

Published 1983
 Second printing — January 1984
 Third printing November, 1984
 Fourth printing May 1985
 Fifth printing March 1986
 Sixth printing January 1987

LANCELOT PRESS LIMITED, Hantsport, N. S.
Office and plant situated on Highway No. 1, 1/2 mile east of Hantsport

APPLE PIE

A   apple pie
B   bit it
C   cut it
D   divided it
E   et it
F   fought for it
G   got it
H   had it
I   eyed it
J   jumped it
K   kicked it
L   longed for it
M   mourned for it
N   nodded at it
O   opened it
P   peeped at it
Q   quartered it
R   run for it
S   snatched it
T   turned it
U   wanted it
V   vowed at it

WXYZ   and John Besant run around the corner with a quarter in his hand.

— oral recitation by Mrs. Grace Williams, 86, of Lockeport, N.S., taught to her when she was a girl by her aunt Effie Williams.

CONTENTS

PREFACE

Whatever may be the truth in the tangled questions of the advantages of city and country life, the greater focus available in one, the confusion and distraction of the other; the jaded, frenetic pace of the one, the boredom of the other; the variety of one, the freshness of the other; one thing seems certain: in the country, language is a primary form of entertainment and a means to enjoy and preserve an oral folk culture. It is especially so because in the country, entertainment has not yet entirely been given over to movies, television, and radio; communication of essential information has not entirely been computerized; and it has fallen to language — the language of everyday speech — to preserve this culture. I think this has happened because the schools have largely chosen to defend a narrow definition of culture (e.g. insisting on the correctness of "this is *he*") and have all too often been compromised by their collaboration with money, class, and politics. What was left? The way we talk.

In the city, people talk to get the point across quickly and get on to the next appointment. The language of the city shows the homogenizing, neutralizing effect of radio, television, and the natural accommodation of millions of strangers to each other when they are thrown together and have to be quickly intelligible to one another. It's what sociologists call "deracination," the loss of roots. An older way of seeing this process would say we've been disinherited; we've sold our birthright for a mess of pottage; we're all exiles. Some say home was the old country from which our ancestors made more or less forced moves, long ago; some say it goes right back to the Garden of Eden, from which we were all expelled by an angel with a two-edged flaming sword; what we all have in common is a feeling of dispossession. But people in the country have generally been dispossessed less recently, and they hang on longer to old ways, of living, and especially of speaking.

For ten years now I have been fascinated by the variety and complexity of the spoken English used along the South Shore of Nova Scotia, a fairly self-contained and isolated piece of country coastline. Here, strung out along one road between Halifax and Yarmouth, villages settled by people from Cape Cod, Boston, New York, South Carolina, Germany, and many other places have been relatively unchanged for up to two hundred years, and the language they use is special. Born an American, now a new Canadian, an Anglophone from Montreal, above all, a person *not from around here*, I have found that my alien ear helps me to recognize the uniqueness of this voice. Those who have lived here all their lives find it perfectly natural.

What did I find, as I began to collect the odd words and phrases I heard and give their meanings and linguistic histories? I found on the South Shore a variety, a complexity of the spoken language, in which it carries warmth and entertainment and wisdom, among perfectly ordinary people, to an extraordinary degree. I found in it an amazing paradox: people are encouraged by one another to use inventive, original expression, and they find also continuing comfort and meaning in old expressions which in the city would long ago have been overused in vague contexts and then discarded as outworn cliches. There is, in short, a balance here which illustrates T.S. Eliot's catch-phrase for the highest poetry, "tradition *and* the individual talent."[1]

This habit, not confined to maritime country areas but

It is interesting to note that Léandre Bergeron makes a similar claim for the French spoken in Quebec in the introduction to his new *Québécois Dictionary* (Toronto: James Lorimer, 1982).

especially noticeable there, has been explained in one way by George Putz in an essay titled "The Ocean: Full Wilderness, Empty Wilderness":

> Maritime people are subject to storms that appear for no known reason and destroy all they have, or are confused by fish that are one year abundant and the next year inexplicably gone. Because of this, they don't try to predict or control their environment, but rather move through it with survival skills based on a combination of handed-down folk savvy and improvisation.
>
> (*Co-Evolution Quarterly*, Fall, 1979), p. 4.

Here, men call each other "old dear." An older man addresses a younger, no longer a youth, as "old son." A married woman, protesting that single women are taking away jobs from married, asks, "What are we supposed to do, stay home and *shovel smoke?*" The language is full of colourful metaphorical, proverbial phrases. A body-shop man, peering under the fender of my old van, says, "Yes, it's getting a bit *tender* under there." I telephone a friend, and his wife says, "No, he's not here; he's out with the Captain," and I know the Captain is Captain Morgan Rum. A man at an auction who can't read or write tells me about a woman he knew who couldn't count, but she used a rhyme to keep track of of numbers — "knit one, purl one, 'tis one, 'taint one, bye and bye" — a rhyme which, derived from knitting, gave her a five-based system, not our decimal system but a folk variation like, perhaps, the binary language of the computers.

A lot of the unusual variety of language here is related to the work on the sea or in the woods or at the quilting club. We use "fired it overboard" to say we throw anything away, whether from boat, truck, or house. "Anchor ice" and "makin' channel" are phrases from the traditional work of logging, and are defined by Thomas H. Raddall of Liverpool, on the South Shore, in his short stories about the area. A lot of phrases have to do with weather: when the loons are "flyin' and cryin'," it's a sign of rain, and it rhymes, just to help enjoy and remember it.

The language is personal. People end lots of phrases

and sentences with "you" ("look, it's some hot, you, and I'm goin' home right now, you"); it's rhythmic punctuation for the sentence, and it establishes a personal contact. It also sounds very like a Welsh syntactic structure ("look you, man"); so it may be a preservation of an old way of talking from across the sea. In fact, I have found considerable evidence that current phrases in use on the South Shore have descended from the language of Renaissance England, through dialects of northern England and New England. Certainly, too, the Lunenburg name for dried apple slices, "snits," owes something to the German word for "to cut," "schneiden."[2] And yet many are new: when people in Port Mouton call driving down the road recklessly "woe-bawling," they may be altering the word "wobbling," but they are making the word itself wobble in an inventive way.

So I've been writing down these unusual common phrases, and have put together this small dictionary. Two cautions: not every phrase is unique to the South Shore — some occur in similar or related form elsewhere in the Maritimes, Newfoundland, or elsewhere in the country areas of North America. And the village names I've attached to many phrases show only where I've encountered them, not where they solely occur.

Outside the cities, we stand in a special relation to the modern age. Visitors to the South Shore, for example, usually see the past in it: they get flashes of nineteenth-century clipper-ship people and things, eighteenth-century ways of living. Much of the natural beauty seems untouched by the twentieth century urban sprawl. Even the new highways, cutting across uninhabited and perhaps uninhabitable barrens, are

2. For a historian's explanation of this phenomenon, see Louis Hartz, *The Founding of New Societies* (New York: Harcourt, Brace & World, 1961), p. 3: "When a part of a European nation is detached from the whole of it, and hurled outward onto new soil, it loses the stimulus toward change that the whole provides. It lapses into a kind of immobility."

uncrowded, uncluttered, and useful, as the first freeways were in the 'forties, leaving the old roads to the oxen, bicycles, and slow drivers.

But this way of seeing the place is not totally shared by the people who live here. Many a fisherman, though he may know the rocks in his harbour well, and all the old ways, is keenly interested in different brands of loran, radar, and sonar gear. They make his life safer. And the men and women ashore enjoy the blessings of some of modern technology: snowmobiles, microwave ovens, ionization-process smoke detectors (useful if you burn wood!), colour television, shopping centres, direct-distance dialing, acid rain.

Mercifully, Nova Scotia is still almost totally surrounded by cold water; the fog is thick and regular; not everyone has taken a commuting, nine-to-five job; nor has everyone forgotten how to play fiddle, chop wood, tell old stories, or talk in the old colourful, elaborate way.

Drying cod at Clark's Harbour, Shelburne Co., N.S.

WORDS AND PHRASES

able — strong, capable, courageous. "A fellow beat up three Mounties in Prince Edward Island. He was some Jesus able, you!" — Port Medway. A woman, too, may be able: see Marilyn MacDonald's column in *Atlantic Insight*, June, 1980. This use of this word is listed by the Oxford English Dictionary as "obsolete," with the meaning "having general physical strength, strong, vigorous, powerful."

aboard — to "go aboard of" someone is to be aggressively angry with him. "I'll fly aboard o'ye and dance a jig on yer palate" is a Cape Sable Island elaboration of this phrase. Ruth C. Lewis in an essay "Why Did You Say That?"[1] on the antiquity of Barrington area English, defines it as "scolding" and cites its use in nineteenth century New England and in Shakespeare (in *The Taming of the Shrew*, "I'll board her, though she chide as loud as thunder"). In the lines from Shakespeare, I suspect a multiple pun on the word, with sexual connotations, but the primary meaning is the same as in the current Cape Island use. In Blanche, Shelburne County, a man said to me, "I gave the dog a bone, and in a couple of seconds she was going aboard of that," using it to mean any vigorous, aggressive behaviour. This expression has of course had wide nautical use for a long time, in the phrase "to go aboard a ship," but its old meaning seems likely derived from the pirate or man-o-war's crew's "boarding" a vessel attacked.

to have **a big sweat** on — to perspire. — Port Medway.

to have **a bun** on — to be drunk. — Port Medway.

to have **a long face** on — to be sad. — Port Medway.

advertised — "When a man puts a notice in the paper that he will no longer be responsible for his wife's debts, they say that she has been *advertised*." — from Ruth C. Lewis' "Why Did

---

1. *Nova Scotia Historical Quarterly*, (Vol. 10, No's. 3 & 4), December, 1980, p. 273.

You Say That?" She also notes that it was used in England as early as 1475 to mean "warning," surely a related meaning.

aglish — "She felt aglish." — Lunenburg. "She felt sick to her stomach."

airin' up — "breezing up," a way of saying that the wind has started to blow. — Shelburne.

anchor ice — also known as *ground ice*, this rare and specific Northern coastal phenomenon is explained by Thomas H. Raddall of Liverpool in the short story "By Any Other Name," in *Tambour and Other Stories*:

" 'cause it forms on the bottom of streams. Usually makes on a clear night — with a temperature 'round zero and a bit of wind. Never forms where the surface is frozen — but just above our pond is a long stretch of rapids, too rough to freeze....It grows on the bottom, like a fungus, grey stuff, soft and spongy-looking. Grows there all night, masses of it. At the first crack of daylight it lets go and comes down the stream — some of it comes to the surface and turns to real ice — contact with the air, d'ye see; stuff like white clinkers. The rest remains in suspension, turning the river to a sort of cold grey soup."

anger knot — a wen, a lump on the neck. — Shelburne.

ashen sail — "He's under an ashen sail." — Shelburne. This is an elaborate metaphorical way of praising someone for working hard to get where he's going. His sail is made of ash, i.e. oars; he's rowing himself. It compares with "he's paddling his own canoe."

auction gale — equinoctial gale. One man explained the name by saying that the big storms which come on the turn of season (the solstice) are so bad that after some "you may as well sell up and move out." — New Germany.

auk-du-leva — expression of surprise or sympathy, an exclamation. I believe it to be a transliteration into English of the German "Ach, du lieber!" ("Oh, my dear!") — Lunenburg.

away — anyplace other than Nova Scotia, usually employed

14

as the direct opposite of "around here": "Are you from *away*? Ye're not from around here." See also **home**.

backing — when appled to weather, used to describe the movement of rain, a storm, high winds, or a disturbance of any kind, in a counterclockwise direction, swinging east to north. Weather travelling in a clockwise fashion, from east to south toward west, is said to be **hauling in**.

backstays — when the "sun's got his backstays down," it's a predictive sign, an omen, of approaching rain. — Liverpool. See also **drawin' water**. In this part of the world, with prevailing west winds, lines in the sky extending down from the sun generally appear only when weather systems are approaching from the west, thus making this visual display a reliable folk weather predictor. Helen Creighton (in *Bluenose Magic*) records a Blandford form: "The sun drawing her stays."

bad — drunk. "I've got to get *bad* a couple of times this summer!" — Shelburne.

bake-apple — a local name, throughout the Maritimes and Newfoundland, for the cloudberry, fruit of a local low bog-dwelling plant, amber when ripe. The plant has one white flower, and the fruit a raspberry-like taste. It is usually smaller than a crabapple.

balautches — talks a lot. — Lunenburg.

banker — a Grand Banks fishing schooner.

bark a blue breeze — "That dog can bark a blue breeze." — Liverpool. This way of describing angry noise is reminiscent of "curse a blue streak." "Blue" seems to be associated with anger, foul language, and hell. See also **hold till the last blue smoke**.

barnscrapings — euphemism for "manure." — Barrington.

barrens — usually a northern word for "tundra," this word is used in Nova Scotia to describe bogs in which blueberries, cloudberries, low stunted spruce, and mosses grow.

15

on the beach — a way of designating where one belongs in a grand local two-fold classification of human beings: "There are lots of fools at sea, but lots more *on the beach*." — R. McGray in the Shelburne *Coast Guard*, 1975. In some of the South Shore villages, the residents are indeed almost evenly divided between those who go fishing and those who don't, who work at the fish plant, are housewives, or do small-scale farming.

belsnickers — masked and costumed entertainers who tour at Christmas with sacks for treats, using gestures only for communication. An old German tradition. — Liverpool, Lunenburg.

Ben Dodie — On Cape Sable Island, a way of teasing a child who eats a lot — "You eat as much as Ben Dodie." This legendary person many years ago appeared in summers at Clam Point and lived in "a cave-like spot between two rocks and covered with a sail." (*Paper Clip*, Vol. 2, No. 17, Feb. 13, 1981). When he visited local people, he apparently ate a lot.

big-feeling — proud, full of oneself. — Cape Negro. "I can't get involved; you're so big-feeling."

Birch Partridge — local name for the ruffed grouse (Robie Tufts, *Birds of Nova Scotia*, Nova Scotia Museum). Wilder and harder to catch than the spruce grouse.

bishburing — whispering. — Lunenburg. This odd coinage, which sounds very like its English equivalent in the vowels but changes the consonants *wh* and *p*, may be partly explained as the result of the absence in German of both the letter *W* and the aspirated sound *wh*, and the similar changes in the history of Germanic languages (both German and English) of the consonants p and b, so that they were perceived as interchangeable.

seven shades **blacker** than a new-painted hearse — a white South Shore resident describing a black one. There is a substantial black settlement in and around Shelburne, descended from the servants of the 1783 Loyalist settlement, who were located outside the town, in Birchtown.

Black Coot — local name for the common scoter duck. (Tufts, *Birds of Nova Scotia*).

Black-Polls — laughing gulls. Robie Tufts (*Birds of Nova Scotia*) reports that these birds, once plentiful — in fact, they once nested here — are now rare, since many were washed ashore after Hurricane Gladys in 1968, dead.

Black Snow-Bird — local name for the slate-colored Junco (Tufts, *Birds of Nova Scotia*).

blow — a braggart or talkative person, perhaps a liar. "He's the biggest blow in the country" — Barrington Passage. This use of the word is probably related to a similar meaning found in country areas as far away as Texas, where in the early years of this century a person approaching the farmhouse would be invited to "sit down and *blow* a while." The word suggests both "relax, brag if you want, feel expansive," and "rest, by getting your breath back," though in the latter sense it has the connotation that the stranger is a lot like his horse, who would rest after a hard run on the road by blowing, breathing hard. The Oxford English Dictionary lists this meaning of *blow* ("brag" or "boast") as dialectal.

blow its poke — used in answering the question, "Doesn't a dead fish float?" "Only if it's blown its poke." Probably the fish's stomach: " 'I've seen a polluck coming up on the line and there'd be herring and small fish coming out of its mouth. Then out would come the poke.' " — **Paper Clip**, September, 1982.

Blue-bill — greater scaup, a kind of duck. (Tufts, *Birds of Nova Scotia*)

Bluenose — a Nova Scotian, a widely known nickname which was originally no doubt an insult. Various explanations have been advanced for its origin, of which a concise summary occurs in the *Concise Dictionary of Canadianisms:*[2] the blue noses of fishermen who must go out in small boats in bad weather; the bluenose potato; and Sir Charles G.D. Roberts'

2. Gage, 1973.

attribution of the term to the legendary fame of a noted privateer from the province which was easily recognized by the blue cannon in the prow.

boil the kettle — make tea or coffee. In the 1920's children would travel home from Little Port LeHebert School, and "all the teams would gather at Squirrel Valley, where the kettle was boiled for breakfast." — Shelburne *Coast Guard*, 1976.

bonnyclapper — thick milk curds. — Queens County. This word preserves an old form of the somewhat more familiar word "clabber" or "buttermilk." Its source may be Irish (*bainne* — milk, and *claba* — thick). There was in fact an Irish settlement in the eighteenth century at Dublin Shore, Lunenburg County.

boomanickels — bulrushes. — Lunenburg.

boughten — this very old form of the word "bought" keeps the ending now almost everywhere dropped off. "Store-boughten" — Chester.

brash ice — broken-up ice floes. — Liverpool. See also **clinkers**.

I was about to **break together** — Lunenburg. Translation of Greman *zusammenbrechen,* break in pieces, "fall apart."

breeze up — a way of saying that the wind is rising. According to Ruth Lewis ("Why Did You Say That?", *Nova Scotia Historical Quarterly*, Dec., 1980) it was used as early as 1752 in Washington's diaries and widely used in New England in the 1800s and in England.

broomed up — a fencepost or stake which has been driven into the rocky ground with a sledgehammer or heavy rock so many times that the tip is splintered, bent over, or blunted. — Port Joli.

browed up — a way to describe logs piled on two skids, perpendicular to the bank, at the river's edge, in a tier, ready to

18

spill them out at the proper moment into the river for the spring log-drive.

bruddle — lower lip. — Lunenburg. "Don't stick out your bruddle at me. You be mootsen someplace else!" See **mootsen**.

bruttselin — simmering. — Lunenburg. This word *sounds* like simmering.

buck fever — "wanting a deer so bad you shake when you try to shoot." — Hemeon's Head.

bucky — like "buddy" in Newfoundland except not necessarily friendly. "Back off, bucky." — Mill Village.

burnt land savages — people from the Camperdown area, according to one Mill Village youth.

Butternose Coot — common scoter duck. (Tufts, *Birds of Nova Scotia*). On Blanche, this bird is sometimes known as the butter*bill* coot.

what does he call for? — what does the weatherman give as the forecast? (Response: "He's giving northeast winds" or "he calls for ..."). See also **giving, wants,** and **meant**.

came in the fog and left in the morning — said of a man who gets a woman pregnant and then leaves her. — Upper Port Latour.

Camp Thief — nickname for the Gray Jay or Canada Jay. Also known as the **Camp Robber**. — Liverpool. See also **Whiskey-Jack, Carryin' Jay, Carrion Jay**.

Candlemas Day, half your meat and half your hay — this Cape Sable Island rhyme offers a way of estimating how well one is getting through the winter, on or near Groundhog Day (Candlemas Day, February 2). According to C.L. Apperson's *English Proverbs and Proverbial Phrases* (London: Dent, 1929), this piece of folk wisdom is from Norfolk, England, having been traced there as early as 1639, and having been recorded in its present form as early as 1732. It is thus further evidence of the link between Cape Island language and Norfolk suggested by Evelyn Richardson in "From Norfolk to the Hawk," *Dalhousie Review* (1953).

cant-hooks — shorthandled iron hooks used to roll logs in the timber drives down the river to the mills at riverhead. — Liverpool.

Cape Island — local name for Cape Sable Island, Shelburne County. The island has given its name wide currency through its distinctive wooden fishing boat, the Cape Islander, in wide use throughout the Maritimes, very seaworthy, and still built of wood and now often of fibreglass, along the South Shore. It is a local tradition that the boat's design, to make it seaworthy, was based on the shape of the seagull, which rides the waves easily.

out with the **Captain** — euphemism for "out drinking." (The Captain is Captain Morgan Rum). "Where is he? He's out with the Captain!" — Shelburne. This is one of many such ways of saying the same thing; one I heard around St. Margaret's Bay was "he has a problem with his elbow."

Cardigan Town — old name for Welshtown, a settlement up the Roseway River from Shelburne. Cardiganshire is a county in western Wales, its capital Cardigan, and there is a Cardigan Bay.

Carryin' Jay or **Carrion Jay** — local names for the Gray Jay or Canada Jay. Both names are descriptive of habits of this familiar and plentiful bird: it steals (see Camp Thief above), and it eats meat (according to Robie Tufts, *Birds of Nova Scotia*, it would steal bait from traplines). See also **Whiskey-Jack**.

cartwheel — the large old one cent piece. — Shelburne.

cat spruce — short scrub evergreen growing along the shore where taller trees can't survive. — Liverpool. See also **mink spruce**. People in Cape Sable Island say the name *cat spruce* was applied because if you "bring one into the house for a Christmas tree, in a few days it'll smell like you've let the

20

tomcat in!"

catching crabs — said of an inexpert rower of a dory or small rowboat, who puts the oars in the water too deep. See also **prairie sailor**.

chick nor child — a way of saying that someone is very poor: "She doesn't have chick nor child." — St. Margaret's Bay.

chowdered it — "You've really chowdered it" means "You've messed it up." — Woods Harbour. The allusion is to the chopping up of fish, onions, potatoes, etc., to make chowder, the common fish soup of the area.

christer — a person who likes to make trouble. In Maine, a bad storm.

chumming — a fishing technique once widespread in the Maritimes in which one would take pickled herring, ground up and mixed with rolled oats, after it had been let stand in a brine solution until quite oily (until it will "float a potato," one man says), and then throw it over the side of the boat by handfuls to make a tasty "oil slick" downwind or downtide of the boat, to attract fish to one's baited hooks. The bait is called **chumbait**, and the practice is also called **chumfishing**. — Upper Port Latour. This expression is occasionally heard all along the maritime coasts of North America.

clapboard — "The boards that cover the side of a house (sometimes called siding) are referred to as *clapboards* in Nova Scotia and in New England. Restrictions on the price of clapboards are found in 1641 in the records of Salisbury, Massachusetts." — Ruth Lewis, "Why Did You Say That?", *Nova Scotia Historical Quarterly*, December, 1980.

clinkers — broken-up ice floes, also known as *brash ice*. — Liverpool.

cobbing — a beating. — Cape Sable Island. The Oxford English Dictionary lists this term as nautical in origin and now obsolete.

Cockerwitters — people from the Woods Harbour and Shag Harbour area of Shelburne County. The name is derived from "Cockerwit Passage," the narrow strip of navigable water between Woods Harbour and Soloman, Vigneau, and St. John Islands. "Cockerwit" is sometimes "Coquewit," as if it were originally a French word; but Mrs. Marion Robertson, the folklorist and historian of Shelburne, reports that Gilbert Nickerson of Shag Harbour, the man who made the famous "Wreck Chair" of bits of salvage wood from 400 wrecks, said the name was attributable to the sound made in the fall by a local bird, "cock-a-link" or "cocker-wit." Robie Tufts, in *The Birds of Nova Scotia*, identifies the sound as "cock-a-wee" and the bird as the old squaw duck. Ruth Lewis says the word is *kakawegech*, an Algonquin-Micmac word meaning "wild duck." She also cites a French form: *cacaouis*, from Cape Breton, 1853. She points out that the term was no doubt originally an insult, since it compared the "ungainly land waddle of the duck" and the "awkward land-gait of a sailor" but now is used "with some pride." ("Why Did You Say That?", *Nova Scotia Historical Quarterly*, December, 1980.)

codding you — kidding you. — Cape Sable Island. The Oxford English Dictionary identifies this expression as slang and dialectal in the 19th century.

Comb Duck — local name for the King Eider duck, according to Robie Tufts (*Birds of Nova Scotia*) because of the "strange formation of its bill."

come — "I was on the Grand Banks. Come a big storm." It is common in storytelling to make the transition from the past tense to the more vivid present tense by using *come*. The story would continue in the present tense: "Winds are 85, 90 miles an hour. It's blowing nor-east...."

confokturing — talking. — Lunenburg.

Cookie — nickname for the cook on a fishing boat.

cookie breath — said of someone who has lemon extract on his

22

South Shore natives
around 1900

breath, no doubt an expression from Prohibition Days. — Liverpool.

Coot — local name for the scoter duck. (Robie Tufts, *Birds of Nova Scotia*) According to the American dialect survey, this local name is applied to the scoter in Louisiana as well; it may have been carried there by the deported Acadians.

courage — "It was such a dreary day I didn't have the *courage* to go fishing." — Upper Port Latour. This use of the word, involving a situation in which there is no great danger in the weather, only perhaps a depressing effect, suggests the original, root meaning of the word (*Coeur* — "heart" in French).

coys — duck decoys. — Blanche. According to the Oxford English Dictionary, now obsolete and dialectal, it meant in 1634, "a place for trapping ducks or other wildfowl, a decoy," exactly as it does today in this area.

cramp knot — a knot from a tree which one would carry in the pocket in the old days, to keep off or control leg cramps. — Shelburne.

Crane — local, popular name for the great blue heron. — Upper Port Latour.

crazy as Luke's dog — a proverbial metaphor used in Cape Sable Island. It is usually completed by, "and he died barking at the moon." I have not found anyone who knows who Luke was, but all believe he was a real person with a crazy dog.

creeter — Cow. — Barrington Passage. This word is similar to the western "critter," a derogatory word for cattle or other farm animals.

crocus bag — burlap bag. — Little Harbour. This usage is common also in England and New England. It preserves the memory of a coarse flaxen cloth known as "crocus" — hence the metaphor "coarse as crocus". (see Alice Morse Earle, *Home Life in Colonial Days*).

cruelize — "This word is used to indicate treatment that is

24

cruel. It is used in the mid-nineteenth century in New England and in England." — Ruth Lewis, "Why Did You Say That?", *Nova Scotia Historical Quarterly*, December, 1980.

crunk — "sick." — Lunenburg. This word is of course the German word for "sick," "krank," transliterated almost exactly into English.

crupp — old past tense form of "cripple." — Blanche. "I crupp him, but he div" ("I crippled him but he dived"). This word, from Old English *crypel*, became in this past tense form confined to the spoken informal dialect in late middle English, following the analogy of "drink" — "drunk."

come a daisy onto it — "pull hard, hit hard, push hard" something. — Chester.

crows — "One crow is sorrow, two crows is joy, three crows a letter, four crows a boy, five crows silver, six crows gold, seven crows a secret never to be told." — Port Medway.

cure — "That man's a *cure*!" means he's from good folks, a dependable neighbour. — Bridgewater.

dancing beggars — originally, people from Shelburne, a term of derision applied by people from the older settlement in nearby Barrington. Evelyn Richardson, the lighthousekeeper's wife who wrote *We Keep A Light* and won the Governor General's Award for it in 1945, explains:

> Barrington, perhaps a little jealous, and not without some justification, of the money and care expended upon the new town, and scandalised at the gay goings-on among the wealthier refugees and the officers of the British men-of-war in harbour, sneered at the "dancing beggars" and prophesied dire ruin.

— "From Norfolk to the Hawk," *Dalhousie Review*, 1953.

Another explanation current in the area is that the early Shelburne settlers, wealthy people from Boston and New York, could not farm or fish, and the few who stayed more than one year after the initial settlement were reduced to tattered, though fun-loving, ne'er-do-wells, given to theatricals and parades. Hence the Barrington **dryhanded**ness (which see). The "Dancing Beggars" label is now proudly borne by Shelburne's summer street theatre troupe.

darken the light — to turn out the light. — Liverpool.

Deacon — the black-backed gull. — Port Medway. See also **Preacher**.

dear dyin' Moses — exclamation. — Little Harbour.

devil-catching — a child's naughty mischief. — Cape Sable Island.

devil's fire — phosphorescent diatoms (algae) which make the water glow with eerie brilliant green light.

Digby chicken — "Like the Frenchman said, the herring before they take the heads off and the guts out." — Shelburne.

dinging — a beating. — Cape Sable Island. This meaning for this word is attributed by the Oxford English Dictionary to dialectal usage in East Anglia.

div — old past tense form of "dive." — Blanche. "I crupp him but he div" ("I crippled him but he dived"). This word, from Old English *dufan*, "to dive," and also from Old English *dyfan*, "to immerse," followed in Middle English colloquial usage the analogy of *bite-bit* and *hide-hid;* and it is the Middle English usage that has survived here, rather than the subsequent mainstream past tense form "dived."

divel a bissle — mild Lunenburg profanity. From German "teufel ein bissel" — the devil a bit.

do-less — a person inclined to be lazy. — Shelburne.

dollop — "A dollop is a rough measure, particularly of things that are spooned into a recipe, like molasses or butter. Its origin is obscure, but it may be related to the Norwegian word

26

dolp meaning *lump*. It is used in New England and in England through the nineteenth century." — Ruth Lewis, "Why Did You Say That?", *Nova Scotia Historical Quarterly.*

dory plugs — thick molasses cookies. — Cape Sable Island.

doughty — said of wood which has been cut and allowed to sit unburned until it begins to rot. — Jordan. See also **dozey.**

dozey — "When wood lies and rots it is said to be getting *dozey*. It is a word associated with Northamptonshire and Warwickshire in England, and with New England. Its use is first noted in the late nineteenth century." — Ruth Lewis, "Why Did You Say That?", *Nova Scotia Historical Quarterly,* Dec., 1980.

draling — a way of fishing. "A 'drale' is a halfmoon-shaped piece of metal, possibly two or three feet long. It has lines and hooks attached to it, each with little wooden pegs resembling bait. As the boat is kept moving, the drale is towed behind it, and the fish bite into the pegs. A drale is known to the fishermen as a Christmas tree, because of all the dangling pieces." — *Paper Clip,* Ingomar, 1980.

drawin' water — a peculiar application of this phrase is an old way of describing what is happening when the sun is out and visible streaks in the sky point toward it, a sign of coming rain. "The sun's a-drawin' water." — Baccaro. See also **backstays.**

drifting — a way of fishing, at night, in which with nets trailing behind, the boat is let drift so that the net is into the tide to intercept schools of fish. — *The Paper Clip,* Ingomar, 1980.

dry-handed — "during the ensuing period of growth and change Barrington began to consider itself the seat of learning and to look down its nose somewhat at the outer villages, which in turn accused Barrington of becoming 'dry-handed' and altogether too high-minded as it turned from fishing to business and the land." — Evelyn Richardson, "From Norfolk to the Hawk," *Dalhousie Review,* 1953.

ducking — duck-hunting. — East Green Harbour. See also **gunnin'**. "An old man who boarded in our village used to take me ducking." — Burns Williams, carver of duck decoys, tells how he started. This meaning for this word is listed by the Oxford English Dictionary as occurring in Richard Hakluyt's *Voyages* in 1577.

dulbatschy — awkward in gait. — Lunenburg. From German *toll batschig.*

dungeon — "a dungeon of fog." — Lockeport. This phrase is only one of many which describe the truly magnificent sieges of fog encountered by visitors to and residents of the South Shore, especially during June and July. It is actually quite clear during the fall, and frequently in the months of January and February. Another description of the texture of fog occurs in Peter Barss' excellent book *Lunenburg County* in the reminiscences of an old fisherman: "It was t'ick of fog, black t'ick of fog."

dutch mess — a dish from Lunenburg County — cod, pork scrap, onions, and potatoes. "Dutch" is of course a transliteration of "Deutsch" or the German word for "German," not Dutch.

dyhinker — mild Lunenburg profanity. From the German "teufel" (devil) and "hinker" (hangman).

a face like a dyin' calf — to describe someone who is melodramatically depressed.

dyin' ol' dyin' or **dyin' holy dyin'** — A curse or exclamation. — Chester. Like a number of oaths heard in this area, this may refer indirectly to the death of Christ on the cross and thus retain the characteristically Elizabethan blasphemous or sacrilegious tinge of many of those in Shakespeare's plays. See also **holy old twist**.

emptying — raining. — Lunenburg. "It's emptying out."

ever — used as an intensifier, in "ever hot," "ever pretty," "ever some pretty."

an eye like a stinking eel — Shelburne phrase to describe the look of someone with a very cold and hostile demeanor.

eyestone — small round stone "used to remove foreign bodies and irritants from the eye. They reside in a ... bed of brown sugar .... They resemble split pea halves .... To determine whether the stones are 'alive' they are placed in a shallow dish of vinegar ... prior to use. If they commence to move around they are deemed 'alive' and are placed under the eyelid of the suffering individual. [They] attract and engulf the irritant and take it with them when they are removed." — from Ron and Joy Laking in *Rural Delivery*, Port Joli, August, 1980. For more information about eyestones see the September, October, and November, 1980, issues of *Rural Delivery*, in which various letter-writers describe them variously as "tiny shellfish" and (from a printed source in Cheshire, England, in 1597) as "seeds." They seem to turn up in Nova Scotia because they were "brought from some far-off place in sailing-ship days."

fachent — withered. — Lunenburg.

fakrupt — someone who has seen better days, down on one's luck. — Lunenburg.

Fall Gull — black-legged kittiwake. — Robie Tufts, *Birds of Nova Scotia.*

faluttle — mislay something. — Lunenburg.

faster than the mill-tails of hell — proverbial, metaphorical way of describing speed, which owes something to the nineteenth-century water-wheels and mill-races in the river-mouths of the South Shore. — Cape Sable Island.

father's t'other end — a room built by the father on the end of the house for a newlywed son or daugther. — Barrington.

fausty — old, moldy, withered. "Have a piece of fausty cake, you." — Lunenburg.

ferdutzt — confused. — Lunenburg. German *verdutzt*, "vexed, chagrined."

fetch it to me — "bring it." — Little Harbour.

fetched a heave onto him — "pulled him" e.g. aboard the boat. — Port Latour.

feed the gulls — be seasick. — Upper Port Latour.

fig — a plug of tobacco. — Liverpool. From Thomas Raddall's story "Wings," "All I can offer you right now is a chaw off my fig o' tobacco."

fine — the only standard and universal word used to describe a day on the South Shore with good weather. It occurs often in the sentence "It's meant to be fine." (see **meant**) It is prominent in the proverbial generalization about the weather: "They say there's one fine day a year in Nova Scotia, and that one's a weather-breeder." — Upper Port Latour.

finest kind — a multi-purpose optimistic phrase much used in some villages and not at all in others. It is to be found as far south as Maine, but nowhere does it have so many uses as along the South Shore. It is a response to "How are you?" "Finest kind." — Upper Port Latour. It may be used to describe a motor: "I changed the spark plugs in her and then she ran the finest kind." — Clyde River. It occurs in the variants "finest o' kind." — Little Harbour — and "like the best o' the kind" and its surely related to the familiar country expression encountered in many places in North America — "finest kind of people."

fire in the wind — trouble, controversy, anger. "There's fire in the wind over this issue." — from the Shelburne *Coast Guard* letters to the editor, spring, 1976 — concerning the bad feeling between inshore (small boat) and offshore (longline, dragger) fishermen over the fishing regulations.

fired it — threw it away, whether from boat, house, or car. "Fired it overboard" is often heard. — Little Harbour

first end, last end — "Down here they talk about things being either at the 'first end of the road' or 'toward the last end of the road.' Lots of roads dead-end up in the woods or out on points of land, so they can in fact have first (at the highway) and last ends. But before there were highways?" — from Dirk van Loon, editor, *Rural Delivery*, Port Joli.

first going off, last going off — a way of describing the birth and death of a child who died young.

Fish-Hawk — local name for the osprey. — Port Latour.

fish-store — shed near the wharf, for storing gear for fishing. Also called "the buildin'." — Port Medway.

flashed up — drunk and happy. — Little Harbour.

flew — On hearing that one long-time resident of the peninsula was about to marry another thirty years his senior, one of the women in the quilting circle recalled, "We were so surprised we almost *flew*." Compare the old gospel song, "I'll fly away, O Glory!"

flutterbug — a person easily excited. — Lunenburg.

flyin' and cryin' — when the loons are "flyin' and cryin' " it is a sign of rain. — Barrington. This rhyming proverb is one of many which contain weather wisdom. For example, "Saturday's rain will never see Sunday noon," (a reference to the frequent changeableness of weather on the coast); and "birds singing for rain" or "robins calling for rain."

fog — "Fog eats ice, burns snow, and breaks the back of winter." This proverbial and metaphorical expression suggests some benefits of fog, otherwise much cursed. Fog, it's said, makes it warmer, and in fact the regular appearance of fog in May and June does signal the end of the cold.

fog breeze — one which blows fog in from the sea. — Clark's Harbour. This phrase is mentioned in Helen Creighton's *Bluenose Magic*.

Natives of region where speech is distinctive
around 1900

fog mull — "a low-lying fog without wind." — Clark's Harbour. In Helen Creighton's *Bluenose Magic.*

fogeater — the sun. — Shelburne. As the sun burns through fog, evaporating the moisture which causes it, it does appear to eat the fog.

it'll be a foggy Friday when I do that — said of something one is unlikely to do. — Barrington Head.

Fool Hen — spruce grouse, so called because it is so easy to catch by hand. — Robie Tufts, *Birds of Nova Scotia.*

foolish — crazy, having taken leave of one's senses. This local meaning for this word is much closer to its meaning in the plays of Shakespeare than to the modern urban meaning of "ignorant" or "imprudent." It may be used of people or animals: in a report in the Shelburne *Coast Guard* on the viewing of a UFO, one person wrote, "It sent the dogs foolish."

fooser — lint. — Lunenburg.

forelaying — expecting, preparing for, or way-laying. — Cape Sable Island. "I'll be forelaying for you." The Oxford English Dictionary calls these meanings (which it dates from 1548 and 1605) now obsolete except in dialectal use. The South Shore use is the same as it was in F, Davidson's *Poetical Rhapsody* (1619): "Privy snares my foes forelay." (II, 361)

fotched — fetched, was taken with, in "He fotched the awfullest flu." — Cape Sable Island.

free-hearted — generous, vivacious. "She's some free-hearted." — Blanche. The Oxford English Dictionary lists this meaning as occurring as early as 1398.

fress — eat, especially in a sloppy way. — Lunenburg. This word was imported directly from German in which it refers to the way animals eat (*fressen*) as opposed to the way civilized people eat (*essen*).

fushlen — fooling around, feeling around. — Lunenburg. This word probably derives from a similar-sounding German word meaning "to move one's feet quickly about, to shuffle," perhaps even "to play footsies."

fussy — often used ironically, as in "I asked a guy working as a dynamiter's helper on a highway construction project: 'How do you like your job?' 'I'm not too fussy about it,' he said." This use of the word is just like that in W.O. Mitchell's Saskatchewan novel *Jake and the Kid.* It sometimes means literally "I don't like it." Its negative uses are probably related to "to make a fuss over" something.

gabalash — to lash a quilt into a quilting frame with big stitches, so that the precise, tiny stitches of the quilting itself may be done by the women sitting around the frame. "I can't gabalash it unless you pass me the string." — Cape Sable Island. It may be used to poke fun at someone's careless or unskilled quilting stitches: "You're just gabalashing it!"

gale — a windstorm. "We were going to take the Bluenose [in this case, the ferry across the Bay of Fundy to Bar Harbour, Maine] but it was blowin' a livin' gale of wind." — Upper Port Latour. Around Little Harbour, people speak of the August gale, a reference to the high winds that come as the year's first hurricane from the South Atlantic sweeps up the coast, usually diminishing in force as it moves.

gall of the government — "That man has the gall of the government!" — Clyde River. This area is known for its individualistic, anti-government sentiments, a tradition which according to Thomas H. Raddall (in the story *At the Tide's Turn*) goes back to the earliest days of the present settlement when, though settled by Loyalists and committed to "Lor an' Order," it was buffeted about by British Navy, American privateers, and Central Canadians, none of them "from around here."

eat like Gannets — Cape Sable Island way of describing children who gulp their food, like the long-necked birds who swallow small fish whole.

34

get ahead — "get moving." — Upper Port Latour. In the local sense, this phrase has none of the abstract urban connotation of upward social mobility. It owes more to the nautical meaning of "go ahead," which means "to propel the boat forward," and is often used to end a casual conversation: "Got to get ahead."

get sick — to go into labour, at childbirth. "She was supposed to get sick last Thursday." — Barrington.

gimp — a cripple, someone who limps. The Dictionary of American Slang shows this word as having been used in the past but now calls it "dialectal." — Liverpool.

givin' — "What's he givin'?" — Little Harbour. This question has only one meaning: "What's the weather forecast?" See also **meant**, and **calling for**. This use may derive from the German *es gibt* ("it is") or *was gibt* ("what is it?").

glin — "sunny pocket in a blanket of fog." — Cape Sable Island. (from Evelyn Richardson's "From Norfolk to the Hawk," *Dalhousie Review* [1953]). This word may be derived from a verb with a similar meaning, "glinter," from 1851. Helen Creighton quotes a Bon Portage Island weather rhyme: "A southern glin/ for a wet skin." (*Bluenose Magic*)

going into one — "getting really angry." — Shelburne.

going like greased lighnin' thru' a gooseberry bush — to describe someone moving fast. — Tancook Island.

going up fool's hill — a person fifteen to eighteen years old. — Shelburne.

gookemole — "Look at this." — Lunenburg. From the German "gucke einmal," "look once" or "just look."

grassin' — "spooning" or "petting." "We went grassin' up on skin hill." — Lockeport. See also **skin**.

green as gall — from Barrington.

groaner — a type of buoy with an eerie "groaning" sound

produced by a bellows, moved up and down by the action of the ocean swells. "Groaner" buoys are offshore, outside each harbour or bay entrance; bell buoys are at the entrances.

ground sea — long, slow breakers, with backwash (undertow). — Liverpool. Also known as *ground sweep*. This phrase with this meaning is listed by the Oxford English Dictionary as having occurred as early as 1642. Both phrases lend considerable vividness to the more familiar but trite inland metaphorical expression "ground swell," as in "a ground swell of support."

ground-sluicin' — shooting at a bird on the ground, rather than in true sporting fashion, on the wing. The expression teasingly suggests that the inexpert hunter is actually digging a ditch with his bullet. — Liverpool.

growlers — big chunks of even bigger icebergs, so called because the edges of cracks grind and rumble. I have heard it said that it was a growler that the *Titanic* struck. — Liverpool.

not fit for Gull's bait — a worthless person. — Cape Sable Island. Who would want to catch a gull anyway?

gunnin' — duck-hunting. "Goin' gunnin'." See also **duckin'**.

gurry — waste from cleaning fish. This word may be an adaptation of the British word *gurry*, which means "diarrhea." A slightly older local meaning for this word is "the cod-liver oil skimmed off the top of a bucket of cod livers which have been allowed to stand for some time."

gush — mouth. — Lunenburg.

gut a swilla — a Lunenburg exclamation. From the German "Gottes wille!" — "May God's will be done!"

hackmatack — local name for the tamarack, or larch tree.

Hags — greater shearwater, a sea bird. Also called *haglins*. — Robie Tufts, *Birds of Nova Scotia*.

to handle line — to do fish-jigging, using line and hooks, rather than using nets or "trawl", a long line set out between buoys with a series of lines and hooks dangling from it. Fishing in this way is known as **handlinin'**.

handspike — spike with a six-foot shaft, for manipulating logs in river timber drives. — Liverpool.

happy as a clam at high water — surely the original of the (incomplete) familiar cliché. A clam would not be happy at low tide. — Upper Port Latour.

haul — to pull on. "Haul a line" means "to pull a rope" and is a familiar nautical expression common all along the North American coast. Here it is applied to any pulling of anything. To "haul a boat" means "to pull it up out of the water onto the shore," usually with a winch or by several men and boys, using rollers (logs) as skids.

hauling in — a weather term, used to describe the shifting of an east wind round to south to get to west, clockwise. Some weathermen call this "veering," but both are to be distinguished from **backing** (which see).

your head doesn't give your feet much work — said to someone who has just made a careless or absentminded mistake. — Blanche. It is also said that one's head doesn't give one's hands, etc. much work.

headin' — to make the twine mesh funnel of a lobsterpot. See **knittin'** and **pothead**.

headworks — special set of machinery, supports for windlass, used to haul logs (towed in rafts and with round booms) ahead to an anchor, progressively throwing anchor ahead, to cross a lake during the timber drive down the river systems and lake-chains. — Liverpool.

heel-spoon — a shoe-horn. — Blanche.

heesik — devout. — Lunenburg.

herring scales — the tiny old five-cent pieces. — Shelburne.

heslik — ugly. — Lunenburg. From the German *häszlich*, "ugly."

high sky — Lunenburg expression — "The window's up high sky."

highliner — fisherman who lands the most fish. — Woods Harbour.

hippling — limping. — Lunenburg.

hoedunker — sweet fruit tart made with leftover pie dough. — Ingomar. This word is remarkably similar to "hoecake," the word used in the American Southwest for a small sweet treat made with leftover pie dough sprinkled with brown sugar and baked briefly in the oven until brown.

hold till the last blue smoke — assurance offered by an expert workman as he tightens down the bolts on the machine he has just repaired: "It'll hold until..." —Pubnico. "The last blue smoke" is, I think, a euphemism for "hell," as in the better known "till hell freezes over."

holy chain lightning — an exclamation. — Chester.

by the holy old dynamiting Jesus — logger's curse. — Liverpool. The elaboration of the curse adds rhythm.

holy old mackinaw — a reference, in an oath, to the plaid jacket worn universally in the woods (and by fishermen). — Liverpool.

by the holy old twist — an oath heard around St. Margaret's Bay. The exact referent of the colourful centre of this expression is not clear, but it may be a rather sadistic and sacrilegious allusion to the Body of Christ on the cross. Such style in swearing is common in Renaissance English; many similar examples may be found in the plays of Shakespeare and Jonson. See also **dyin' holy dyin'**.

38

home — Nova Scotia, especially the immediate area of the speaker, usually in this form: "When did you get *home*?" (asked of everyone, even summer people, whether from "around here" or from "away."

come a horn onto it — to exert extra pressure onto a thing to get it to move, or come unstuck. — Chester.

horse beans — local name for broad beans, for baking. — Reynoldscroft.

housebanken — diced cooked vegetable and pork scrap. — Lunenburg.

hove — to tarry, stay, or dwell in a place. "I hove to" or "I hove up" means, "I stopped," and it is used on land and at sea. The Oxford English Dictionary reveals that the source of this word and meaning are not "heave" as might be expected, but an old word much closer to modern "hover." In 1220 "hove" meant "to remain in a suspended or floating condition, as a boat in the water, to lie at anchor," and it was superseded in general usage by the 16th century by the word "hover." — Blanche. A line from Edmund Spenser's **Faerie Queene** illustrates its Elizabethan use: "A little bote lay hoving her before." (III, vii, 27)

hubble — homemade cabbage slicer/grater for sauerkraut, made of a washboard frame for a knife, over which the cabbage would be passed. — Lunenburg. **Hubbling** is therefore "grating cabbage for sauerkraut." "In bygone days they shredded all the cabbage by hand, pushing each head back and forth across a set of knife blades fixed in a wooden trough." — Thomas H. Raddall, "Happy Island," [Tancook Island] *Macleans*, November 1, 1946.

hungry March — a common way of referring to this month, which comes at a time when winter lingers in the Maritimes. Another description of this time of year is "Long-legged March, starve-gutted April, and up May hill.") — Upper Port Latour.

nunkadory — a chewy, flat, thin coconut-flavoured sweet from the 1890s. — Cape Sable Island.

hutcher — big. — Lunenburg.

hutzelsup — a mess. "It's a real hutzelsup." — Lunenburg. May be named for a soup made of *hutzel* (German for "dried apple" or "dried pear").

iglish — grouchy, cranky, out of sorts. — Lunenburg. May be related to **aglish** (which see).

ignorant — used for a wide range of insulting judgments, not just of someone who lacks information.

imagine — "I imagine" is a very common way to say "yes." — Port Mouton. This use is widespread in the Maritimes; it occurs in this exact sense in *Anne of Green Gables*, Lucy M. Montgomery's perennial best-seller about Prince Edward Island.

into it — "after insulating, you wouldn't believe the difference into it." — Cape Sable Island. It has the effect of an intensifier. See also **onto it**.

in — back to the wharf or anchorage from **outside** (which see). — Port Joli. "Somebody told of an experience out on the banks and said that at such and such a time they pulled in their gear and *left for in.*" (Dirk van Loon, editor of *Rural Delivery*).

it — the essence of anything, as in "That's the *it* of it." — Bridgewater.

jakey — Jamaica ginger, a fruit-flavoured, alcoholic drink consumed along the south shore during Prohibition. — Port Latour. See also **tutti-frutti**.

jib — "Other than its use to describe a triangular stay-sail, *jib* is sometimes used to describe a small irregular piece of land, especially a triangular piece such as one that might be cut diagonally out of a squared field by a road or a stream." — Ruth C. Lewis, "Why Did You Say That?"

jinker — one pronunciation of **tinker** (which see), an undersized lobster or fish. — Lunenburg.

doing your job — having a bowel movement. — This meaning is no doubt related to the British euphemism for the same thing, "doing your business."

a good job of work — "I do love a good job of work" — a challenging, physical task.

Joner — Cape Sable Island expression for a "Jonah" or a jinxed (unlucky) car or boat.

kanalee — simple or odd person. — Lunenburg.

kanapp — rattle. — Lunenburg. From the German *klapper* ("rattle")?

kanutch — squeeze. — Lunenburg.

kanuttering — talking to oneself. — Lunenburg.

kanuttle — gather together. — Lunenburg.

ka-stave up — "We stopped ka-stave up" is a Cape Sable Island way of saying "we stopped suddenly."

kashittery — "What a kashittery!" ("What a fuss!"). — Lunenburg. From the German *Geschütterei*, an outpouring of words.

katy-dids — local Barrington name for bulrushes ("cat-tails").

kiack — local name for the gaspereau (French name) or ale-wife (New England name), a smallish bony fish which comes to the shore and runs upriver in large numbers in the spring. Traditionally during the run they are caught by dip-nets at the river mouths; their taste is much improved by a smoke-curing process. — Barrington.

Killy-Willy — local name for the willet. — Barrington.

king pead — local card game in Port Medway, invented and very common there.

kink — a nap. "I got to take a little kink." — Port Joli.

kisibo — funny person. — Lunenburg.

klumpers — big shoes. — Lunenburg.

klutters — diarrhea. — Lunenburg.

knit one, purl one, 'tis one, 'taint one, bye-and-bye — counting rhyme employed by a woman who could not read or write, and did not use the ten-based system we use for counting, but instead this five-based system derived from her knitting. — Villagedale.

knittin — making, by a macramé technique, the mesh funnel for lobster pothead, using two flat wooden or bone (now plastic) needles and twine. — Port Medway.

knuttled — twisted and knotted, e.g. wool. — Lunenburg.

krexy — fussy and complaining. — Lunenburg. "You're always kreksing about something."

krily kripse! — "for goodness sake!" — Lunenburg.

kroppy-doppy! — "my goodness!" — Lunenburg.

kruts — to cut in a crude way. "You'll only kruts it with that dull pair of scissors." — Lunenburg.

krutty — small. — Lunenburg.

kuduffle soup — soup of homemade noodles, potatoes, gravy made with browned flour. From the German *kartoffeln* (potatoes). — Lunenburg.

kutz — vomit. — Lunenburg.

Labrador Robin — in Liverpool, a robin seen in winter.

laid — When four men go duck-hunting and split up into pairs in the duckblinds, one says, "I laid together with Wilmer and Walter laid with Mervyn." They lie down to hide. — Blanche.

42

Sea Gulls around wharf at Kelly's Cove

lambkiller — a severe sudden storm in March, just after lambs are born. — Ingomar.

lank — hungry. "I'm feeling lank." — Clyde River. This unusual occurrence of this old word in everyday speech gives fresh meaning to an old cliché, "lank and lean."

larrigon — footwear for work in the woods, in the old days. "Made like a boot, but had no sole. They were awfully slippery, but good with snowshoes. They were different heights and made by hand by the shoemaker. Sometimes the soles were fastened onto them and they were worn in summer." — Ingomar (The *Paper Clip*, Feb. 13, 1981). See definition in the *Concise Dictionary of Canadianisms*, p. 137.

leeward day — a day when one can't work. — Shelburne. "Leeward" is of course the nautical term (from sailing) which indicates the side of the boat away from the wind. Also known as "a day on the shelf."

lepish — tasteless. — Lunenburg.

linktoe, linktoe, cross so'side vannah, up a tree, down a limb, in a hole, out again, bang bang — Cape Sable Island children's rhyme describing a journey from South Side (So'Side) to Centreville, across the island, across a savannah (a broad, open marshy area). It is a local rhyme comparable to a familiar Boston one: "Trot, trot to Boston, Trot, Trot to Lynn, Trot, Trot to Salem, and Home Again" — or the Newfoundland "Fogo, Twillingate, Morton's Harbour, all around the circle."

lallygigging — Chester version of "lollygagging," used to describe boys' and girls' visits to "lover's lane."

log-brow — tier of logs at river's edge in preparation for log-drive. See also **browed up**.

look for — expect. "I'll be looking for my husband home for supper about then." — Barrington.

loppy — a way of describing the ocean surface when a wind and big sea have made whitecaps (as the wind knocks the tops off the waves.) — Lunenburg. This word is listed by the
44

Oxford English Dictionary as having nineteenth century use. See also **windlop**.

Lord dyin' Jesus — exclamation. — Liverpool.

Lord liftin' — exclamation. — Little Harbour.

Lord thunderin' — exclamation. — Bridgewater.

Lords and Ladies — local name for the Harlequin duck, according to Robie Tufts (*Birds of Nova Scotia*) because of "the elegance of the drake."

Lordy ole Cock-Robin Christ — exclamation. — Lunenburg.

lounder — a hard punch, a generous portion, or a loud clap of thunder. — Cape Sable Island. "Two fellows were driving in the winter slush, and to clean the windshield, they stopped and one put some snow on it. This didn't quite clean it, and so the other one yelled to his friend, 'Throw another lounder on it!' " As early as 1723, according to the Oxford English Dictionary, this word was in use to mean "a heavy blow, to beat, or to hurl with violence on something."

if you love me — "if you please." — Ohio Road, Shelburne County. A fellow I'd given a drive to, when asked where he'd like to be let off, said, "Just by that white house on the right, if you love me."

lunch — an evening snack, usually tea, sandwiches, cake, squares, cookies. Taken at the end of quilting, etc. — Blanche.

Lunenburg champagne — rum. — Liverpool.

Mackerel Gulls — local name for the common tern, which dives near shore for near-surface fish (like the mackerel). According to Robie Tufts (*Birds of Nova Scotia*), their spring arrival is eagerly awaited, "like the robin's." A West Middle Sable fisherman says that their arrival forecasts the arrival of the mackerel; some say they arrive on the same day.

Mackerel sky, never twenty-four hours dry — a mackerel sky is a sky streaked and spotted, and bluish-grey like a mackerel. It is regarded by folk weather-wisdom as a sign of rain or of a change in the weather.

mawger — thin, miserable. — Lunenburg. From German *mager*, "thin." See also **moger**.

making — going. It may be used to describe walking, driving, or travelling by boat. It may be used of the ocean: "The Hawk itself is really an island for a salt inlet *makes* in behind it." — Evelyn Richardson, "From Norfolk to the Hawk," *Dalhousie Review*, 1953.

makin' channel — a term from logging. "The booms coming down the lake, the sluicing, the labor with peavey and pike pole in the rapids below, *making wings of the stranded logs to fend off the rest* — makin' channel, as the river drivers said." — Thomas Raddall, "Sport," *Tambour and Other Stories*. — Liverpool. "And where they've made channel, remember a bunch o' logs can change the whole nature o' the stream — the river squeezed into half its berth, and water pilin' up in a crazy rush where you expect an or'dinary bit o' rapids."

make fish — "Cure" fish by splitting, salting, and drying it, usually outdoors on "flakes" or wooden racks. — Lunenburg. This process is still carried on along the South Shore. According to Thomas Raddall, it had to be done in September, as in July and August, it would "burn" or turn dark. ("Happy Island," [Tancook] *Macleans*, November 1, 1946).

making wet — raining. — Lunenburg.

is it making anything down — is it raining? — Lunenburg.

meant — "had to," "made plans to," "was supposed to" — Upper Port Latour. "is rumored to" — Blanche. "I was meant to be going to Yarmouth on Thursday." "She is meant to be the one who sells eggs."

meringue storm — a storm in which the wind whips sea-foam up off the tops of the waves over the rocks and onto the lawn at the lighthouse, at the end of the peninsula. — Baccaro.

46

metzelsuppe — blood sausage, made immediately after a pig is slaughtered. — Lunenburg.

mink spruce — scrub evergreen which grows near the shore where trees can't grow tall. — Liverpool. See also **cat spruce, scrub spruce.**

moger — wretched or miserable. — Cape Sable Island. (from Evelyn Richardson's "From Norfolk to the Hawk," *Dalhousie Review*, 1953). See also **mawger.**

mollyhawking — destroying. — Chester. "The deer are mollyhawking the apple trees."

monkey-meat — children's name for the small white edible pods or nuts which may be found at the base of the fiddlehead fern, among the roots. — Upper Port Latour.

mootsen — sulking. — Lunenburg. From the German *murrisch* (?), "surly, morose, sulking."

more than somewhat — response to "how are you?" perhaps to express a comparative degree of "somewhat worse" or "somewhat better." — Chester.

motching — messing. — Lunenburg.

mother soul alone — an intensive way of saying "alone." From the German *mutterseelenallein*, "all alone." "Mutterseele" means "human being." — Lunenburg.

mugup — "a shack, particularly one before going to bed, is often called a *mug up.* Kipling used it in *Captains Courageous*, and it is attributed mostly to fishermen in the Grand Banks schooners. It was used in some British dialects in the nineteenth century." — Ruth C. Lewis, "Why Did You Say That?"

muxey — untidy. — Lunenburg.

natter — "When a wife nags her husband she is *nattering*. The word is used commonly in British and Scottish dialects." —

Ruth C. Lewis, "Why Did You Say That?" *Nova Scotia Historical Quarterly*, Dec., 1980.

niddy-noddy — a stick about a foot long, with end-pieces, used to wrap yarn on. — Little Harbour.

nigh — "Nova Scotia's rocky soil and slow economic development have made the horse and the ox a more recent loss than in the areas where tractors plough vast fields without striking rocks. Oxen are still used in small lumbering operations and for competition in ox-hauling contests. The left horse of a team and the left ox of a team are known as the *nigh* horse and the *nigh* ox, because they are guided from the left... The reins are held from the left, probably because the blade of the plough throws to the right." — Ruth C. Lewis, "Why Did You Say That?"

Nightingale — local name for the hermit thrush. — Robie Tuffs, *Birds of Nova Scotia*.

no more luck than a calf, born in winter, died in the spring — Shelburne saying.

Noddy — local name for the razor-billed auk.

nubbins — a young, green hired hand. — Woods Harbour.

off/on — off the mainland, on the mainland.
"I'm going from off to on,
To Barringt'on
Where they've got sugar cookies,
And t'other rooms:"
— Cape Sable Island folk poem
This rhyme dates from before the causeway was built, just after World War II, connecting the island with the mainland. The reference to sugar cookies is notable because the available sweetener on the island at that time was molasses. See **t'other rooms.**

off — when said of the wind, used to describe a wind from the land. — Tancook Island.

off — "The right horse or ox of a team is called the *off* horse, or the *off* ox. Again *off* is farther off, as opposed to *nigh*, near." — Ruth C. Lewis, "Why Did You Say That?" See **nigh.**

off-fall — "Clean the fish and throw the off-fall inta the wata!"

off town/on town — outside/in Lockeport, which is on an island.

oil ca'm — a way of describing a particular calm condition on the sea. It refers to the old trick of pouring oil overboard on a rough sea, to create a calm patch around the boat. — Lunenburg. Inland, we say, "oil on troubled waters," a metaphorical use which has lost all the vividness of its origin.

old Christmas Day — January 6, Epiphany, the last of the twelve days of Christmas. — Port Joli. The Oxford English Dictionary finds this phrase in use in Britain in 1863.

old dear — term of affectionate address between men and women. — Upper Port Latour. Nearer Halifax, a similar term of address which, like this one, is often used between men, is "old diddy."

old man — captain of a fishing vessel, a term used to address him only at sea, and on land used only to refer to him, not to his face. — Shelburne.

old son — term of affectionate address from an older to a younger man, the younger not literally son of the former. — Port Clyde. This term occurs in Robert Louis Stevenson's *Treasure Island*, between Long John Silver and Israel Hands, who is not young. It is comparable to the British "old boy."

old stick or **old sticky** — a sailor. — Liverpool.

on the shore — inshore fishing, near the coast. — Shelburne.

only good on the water — an ironic way to say that a fierce wind is blowing, said from shore, fully aware that the wind is blowing harder on the water. — Barrington.

onto it — intensifier. "A little polish put quite a shine onto it."

outside — in the open ocean. See **in**.

owly — in a bad mood. "She was right owly today." Liverpool.

own horse, own corn — "own fault." — Villagedale. If you let your own horse get into your own corn, you have no one to blame but yourself.

patti-pans — cupcakes (Cape Sable Island). The Oxford English Dictionary dates this usage from 1694, in England.

peansing — trying to cry. — Lunenburg.

peavey — a loggers' tool, made by combining the cant hook and the handspike. The name of the tool has been traced to a Maine blacksmith, the inventor, but around Liverpool, N.S., the "Bangor peavey" was distinguished from the local peavey, which had no metal cap, and in fact two local varieties were known: the "Mersey" with three rings, and the "Medway" with two, named for the two largest local rivers in the Liverpool area.

Peeps — small sandpipers. — Robie Tufts, *The Birds of Nova Scotia.*

phoxed — puzzled. — Lunenburg. "I'm phoxed!"

Pie-Not — local name for the dovekie, a little duck. — Blanche.

pig in a bag — said of something bought sight unseen. This phrase actually clarifies the old cliché "pig in a poke" (In *Oxford English Dictionary* "poke" is Old English for "bag"). — Barrington.

pigeonberry — local name for the bunchberry dogwood.

Pink-Winks — small frogs, known as "peepers" elsewhere. — Barrington.

played out — tired. — Blanche. This popular metaphor, in general use in North America, has here often a sexual

50

connotation: "She's got him all played out."

pleasance — a small rose-garden. — Liverpool. The novelist Thomas Raddall, planting a few rose-bushes in his yard in the 1940s, was greeted by his neighbour with "I see you're making a pleasance." The Oxford English Dictionary finds its first use in 1585, with the meaning "a pleasure-ground, secluded part of a garden:" "Diuers gardens and pleasaunces, planted with orange-trees." (T. Washington's translation of *Nicolay's Voyages*, IV, xxiii, 139).

as pleasant as a bucket of chips — said of a very friendly person. — Villagedale.

pogie — unemployment insurance or welfare. This term, in use throughout the Maritimes, and in depression times in Ontario and the West, is still familiar in Nova Scotia. It was in fact the title of a play by Chris Heide performed by Stages, a Halifax cabaret theatre troupe, in the spring of 1980.

poke — see **blown its poke**.

poor — the dead are always referred to as "poor..." — Blanche.

poor man's fertilizer — Blanche name for a late winter snow. It is also called "poor man's topdressing" and "farmer's fertilizer."

porridge on a limb — an easy pool shot. — Shelburne. "The sixball was lying there like porridge on a limb."

pothead — the twine mesh funnel in the lobsterpot (trap) through which the lobster enters the trap and out of which he cannot go. — Ingomar. See also **headin'** and **knittin'**.

prairie sailor — someone who, when rowing, raises the oars too high on the return stroke, wasting energy and often popping the oars out of the oarlocks, which here are often two wooden pegs, not closed on top. — Baccaro. For someone who dips the oars too deep in the water, see **catching crabs**.

pram — small boat, shallow, fairly-flatbottomed, used for

Lunenburg Fisheries Exhibition

duck-hunting or as tender to a larger boat or yacht. It is usually about eight feet long, often slightly blunt at the bow. — Woods Harbour.

Preacher — Shag Harbour name for the black-backed gull.

on the prod — provoked, aggressively angry. — Ingomar. This phrase appears in the *Western Canadian Dictionary* (1913), recently republished by the University of Alberta.

pulling my mouth — trying to get me to say something. — Cape Sable Island. This expression is modelled on, or an original version of, the more familiar "twisting my arm," "pulling my leg," or the rare "pulling my coat," (pointing out a pretty girl to watch).

quiffy — snooty, "uppity," **dry-handed** (which see). — Lunenburg.

rack — to "rack in a shell," to load a gun quickly. Related to "to place or arrange on a rack", "rack up a score." — Liverpool.

rain before seven, fine before eleven — weather wisdom in folk rhyme. Another is, "if it rains while the sun's out, the devil is beating his wife," a proverb dating from 1666.

rainworm — earthworm. — Lunenburg. This name, which is also found in England, no doubt derives from the fact that the worms come up from under the earth before a rainstorm, making their appearance a sign, or predictive omen, of rain.

rearing the drive — loggers' term, describing the activity of the men who follow the main body of logs as they float down the swollen rivers on the flood caused by the thaw of winter snows inland, prying loose logs caught on the sides and left behind in the main drive. — Liverpool and Barrington.

reise — move. — Cape Sable Island. From Evelyn Richardson's "From Norfolk to the Hawk."

right — very. "Right little," "right smart," "right many." This

53

intensifier is also used in New England and along the Middle Atlantic, to as far away as Louisiana.

rinctum — "an especially violent fit of temper." — Cape Sable Island. (From Evelyn Richardson's "From Norfolk to the Hawk.") "A heavenly rinctum."

Ringneck — local name for the semi-palmated plover. — Robie Tufts, *The Birds of Nova Scotia.*

rivvels — noodles for soup. — Lunenburg. See **roovled**.

rob roy — an outer porch. — Cape Sable Island.

Rock Duck — local name for the harlequin duck, because it "feeds in inshore waters off rocky coastlines." — Robie Tufts, *The Birds of Nova Scotia.*

roovled — wrinkled. — Lunenburg. From the German *runzeln* (?), "wrinkle."

roshplin — travelling. — Lunenburg. From the German *reisen* (?), "to travel."

rout — the noise of the waves on the shoreline, used to determine position in the fog. — Cape Sable Island. "I'm listening for the *rote*. The surf breaks with a different sound all along the shore." — Helen Creighton, *A Life in Folklore*, reporting the conversation of a Cape Sable Island fisherman. This very old word, from Norwegian roots, occurs in Henry Hudson's voyages, reported in the accounts of the Renaissance chronicler Samuel Purchas in *Purchas His Pilgrimes* (1625). The word is used by Hudson himself, by his mate Robert Iuet, and by Abacuk Pricket, one of the seamen who put Hudson adrift in a small boat:

> from Hudson's diary: "Wee heard a great *rutte* or noise with the Ice and Sea....We heaved out our Boat, and rowed to towe out our Ship farther from the danger." from Iuet's diary: "And at ten of the clock we heard a great Rut, like the Rut of the shoare."

from Abacuk Pricket's diary: "on which we fell in a fogge, hearing the Rut of the Sea ashoare, but saw not the Land, whereupon our Master came to an Anchor." — *Henry Hudson's Voyages* (Ann Arbor: University Microfilms, 1966), Bk. III, Ch. 14 of *Purchas His Pilgrimes* (facsimile of 1625 edition), pages 573, 587, 597.

It is particularly interesting that the first two of these entries were made when Hudson was off Newfoundland, and the third when they were sailing down the South Shore, near Cape Sable Island, where the word is still used. Originally from the Old Norse *rauta* ("to roar"), in Chaucer's time this word was already used of the sea, winds, etc.: in *Troylus*, "the sterne wind so loud gan to route that no wight other noyse might here." (III, 743).

ruddle — to slip up. — Lunenburg.

the sea has quite a run on — a strong tidal current. — Jones Harbour.

runzelled — shrivelled. — Lunenburg. From the German *runzelich*, "shrivelled."

rutch — squirm or jostle into position. "Stop rutching around in your seat and pay attention." "It took a lot of rutching to get the piano through the door." — Chester. In Lunenburg, the word means "can't sit still."

santyin' or sandyin' — "Santa-ing," or another word for the Christmas custom of **belsnicking** (which see), especially in the Lockeport area.

savage — very angry. — Port Medway.

savory meat — Thomas Raddall, the Liverpool novelist, says that someone in Liverpool used to go out to the horse-drawn meat cart and ask "Do you have any savory meat today?" This phrase is very old; it is familiar from its use in that popular Elizabethan vernacular translation of the Bible, the King James Version, in the account of the tasks set by Isaac for Esau

55

and Jacob, that they might gain his blessing, in Genesis 27. "Savory meat" here means "treated and aged venison:" "Now therefore take, I pray thee, thy weapons, thy quiver and thy bow, and go out to the field, and take me some venison/ and make me savoury meat, such as I love." (verses 3 and 4) It occurs in this exact form no less than five times in the chapter. That this phrase is peculiarly Elizabethan is clear from a comparison with the more recent translations, where the original is rendered as "the kind of savoury I like" (Jerusalem), "a savoury dish of the kind I like" (New English Bible), and "some of that tasty food" (Good News Bible).

schlapperharniss — a derogatory term, "an old schlapperharniss." — Lunenburg.

schmockelin — hugging. — Lunenburg.

schmuck off — a small bath. — Lunenburg. This phrase is imported from the German, in which two similar sounding words have almost opposite, but related meanings: *schmucken* means "to spruce oneself up," and *schmutz* means "filth, smut, dirt."

schnevilly — pale. — Lunenburg.

schnuddles — leftovers. — Lunenburg.

schnupps — sneezing. — Lunenburg.

schoolmarm — piece of firewood where two trunks have grown together and crossed. So called because "you'll never get them apart." — Blanche. This phrase, "schoolmarm tree" for a tree in the shape of a Y, occurs in Howard O'Hagan's novel of the Canadian West, *Tay John* (1939).

schooner — name used aboard a boat for a pig. On a boat, for superstitious reasons, a pig is never called a "pig," and it is extremely bad luck to put a pig on board.

scluttery — fatty. — Lunenburg. Also, "shaky, like a bowl of jelly." From the German *schlotterig,* "loose, shaky, flabby."

scoffed — stolen, taken. — Chester. From the old nautical use, meaning "seized, plundered."

scouse — pork or beef chowder. — Cape Sable Island. In use in England in the 19th century.

scrub spruce — one of many varieties of low-growing evergreen trees kept from growing straight and tall by the severity of the coastal winds, salt spray, etc. — Liverpool. See also **mink spruce, cat spruce**.

scullywagger — the sculpin, the "ugliest fish in the sea."

scurryfungering — fooling around. — Port Mouton.

Sea Duck — local name for the common eider. — Robie Tufts, *Birds of Nova Scotia*. On Blanche, it is used for the cormorant. (See **Shag**)

Sea Geese — phalaropes. — Robie Tufts, *Birds of Nova Scotia*.

Sea Hawk — parasitic jaeger. — Robie Tufts, *Birds of Nova Scotia*.

sea laws — "predictions of the weather and fishing for the morrow" by men hanging around the post office. (*Paper Clip*, April 29, 1982). — Roseway. This expression surely explains the commonly known "sea lawyer," defined by the *Dictionary of American Slang* as "a sailor who pretends to know more than he does, who is argumentative, free with unwanted advice" (p. 455, ed. Wentworth and Flexner, publ. Crowell). "Sea lawyer" appears in the writings of Herman Melville, the mid-nineteenth century American author of *Moby Dick*.

sea manure — red, feathery seaweed put on gardens to rot and enrich them, also known as rockweed.

there's a sea on — way of saying that the waves or swells are high.

Sea Parrot — local name for the puffin. — Robie Tufts, *Birds of Nova Scotia*.

57

Sea Pigeon — black guillemot. — Robie Tufts, *Birds of Nova Scotia.*

Seaweed Bird — the turnstone, a bird so called because it "turns over small stones to find food along the shore." — Robie Tufts, *Birds of Nova Scotia.*

semiquibber — fool, idiot. — Lunenburg.

Shag — local name for the cormorant.

sheet of cake — a flat cake, like squares, as contrasted with "a loaf of cake" made in a bread loaf pan. — Cape Negro.

Shell-Drakes (Shell Ducks) — merganser ducks. Robie Tufts, *Birds of Nova Scotia.*

getting down to the fine shims — metaphor from mechanics for "getting down to the last stages of bargaining." — Shelburne.

shimmy — a shirt. — Cape Negro. From the French "chemise" ("shirt"), this word was used this way in dialectal areas in England in the 19th century. "Ain't got no petti-skirt, ain't got no shimmy shirt." — Queens County.

shoopie — needs a haircut. — Lunenburg.

shorn — metaphorical use in the proverb, "Many who go for wool come back shorn." — Shelburne. This proverb occurs in print in the Coppernose tales by Peter Harris in *Good Morning*, 1978.

shovel smoke — do housework. In a letter to the editor of the Shelburne *Coast Guard*, a married woman contends that single women are taking away jobs from married, and asks, "What are we supposed to do, stay home and shovel smoke?"

schussley, schushlish — acting silly, giddy, making a fool of oneself. — Lunenburg. This is from the German, directly transliterated into English. **Schuss** is "fool."

schwindely — dizzy. — Lunenburg. From the German *schwindelig*, "dizzy."

shy — "Is he shy? I don't know, but he used to *shy* around with Marge." — Blanche.

sidewheeler — large passenger vessels propelled by a large paddlewheel at the side, used briefly in the late 19th and early 20th centuries as coastal and Fundy ferries. They were probably better suited to Mississippi River traffic: one, the *Monticello*, was wrecked off Yarmouth November 10, 1900, with great loss of life.

sixty twice and thrice is nice — Barrington storekeeper's counting rhyme, as he made change for a five dollar bill on a purchase of $1.40, with sixty cents in change and three one-dollar bills.

getting your skin — used by a male to describe sexual intercourse.

skiwift — cockeyed. "You drop a lobster crate, you know how it'll go skiwift?" "You see a barn leaning, and you say, 'the wind blew it skiwift.' " "You got a crate in the water by the wharf, and the boat goes up against it, squush it skiwift." — Dirk van Loon, *Rural Delivery*, Port Joli.

Skunk-Head Coot — local name for the surf scoter drake, because of its black and white headdress. — Robie Tufts, *Birds of Nova Scotia.*

skutting — hurrying. — Lunenburg.

slankering — walking. — Lunenburg.

slippery side up — after a big rainstorm, the ground is "slippery side up." — Sable River.

smart — active, well. — Cape Sable Island. The Oxford English Dictionary lists this usage as having occurred first in 1340.

smurry — "When the sky begins to cloud as though it might rain, some of our friends who are fishermen say that it looks *smurry*. In the Scottish dialect, a *smurr* is a drizzling rain. The

Scots got the word from the Teutonic *smoor*. It was widely used in Scotland, Ireland, and northern England to the eighteenth and nineteenth centuries, and in New England in the nineteenth." — Ruth Lewis, "Why Did You Say That?"

smutched — smeared. — Lunenburg. From the German *schmutz*, "dirt," "filth," "mud."

smoky sou'wester — a thick, hazy storm, from the southwest. — Barrington.

snits — dried apple slices. — Lunenburg. From the German *schnitten*, "to cut."

snow hole — in Conquerall Banks, when the "wind is in the snow hole," it is "coming in from the sea and bringing snow." — Helen Creighton, *Bluenose Magic*.

snowbanker — a big American car, hard to control on icy and snowy roads. — Port Joli. Also known as a "Yank Tank."

solomon gundy — salmagundi, or salt herring marinated in vinegar, pickling spice, and onion.

some — common ironic use to mean "very," as in "some hot," "some good." Degrees of variation are expressed this way: "good," "some good," "right some good," "right some Jesus good." Murray Kinloch, the linguist of the University of New Brunswick, has identified this use of the word as occurring in Cornwall, Lincolnshire, and Lancashire, in England.

songing — "Otis Purdy got his bills paid by 'songing' his debtors. If they had heard what he sang about them once, he need only begin with "Come all you jolly jokers, listen to my song,' " — Helen Creighton, *A Life in Folklore*. — Baccaro.

sook — crybaby. — Lunenburg. "A sooky baby."

sookied — tired. — Lunenburg.

soonth — the shape, the lines of a boat's hull, judged by eye, not by the precise boatbuilder's guidelines, or *shear* of the

60

shape.

sowff — "always sowffin'," to drink excessively. — Lunenburg. From the German *saufen*, "to booze it up, to guzzle."

spiller — as defined in Helen Creighton's *Folklore of Lunenburg County*, a net to catch fish that fall overboard, used with the "sweep," a big boxlike net that acts as a trap, in albacore (tuna) fishing.

spoke — "I spoke him about three o'clock, off the Half-Moons." — Ingomar. This nautical use of the word occurs both on and off shore, to describe meeting or briefly encountering someone.

spondulicks — money. — Lunenburg. This word, one of many slang terms for money, occurs in the monologues of the American comedian W.C. Fields, as he starts a poker game: "Do you have any of the elusive spondulicks?"

Spot-Rump — local name for the short-billed dowitcher. — Robie Tufts, *Birds of Nova Scotia*.

spritched — splashed. — Lunenburg.

stand there swingin' on the garden gate — "Don't you call me out to go and then stand there swingin' on the garden gate." Hence, to delay departure.

Stake-Driver — local name for the American bittern, because of the male bittern call during mating, described as "like a pump," "like a stake being driven into wet boggy soil," and "like a gulp." — Robie Tufts, *Birds of Nova Scotia*.

stempel — a kind of "giant potato masher" used in compressing shredded cabbage in barrels while making sauerkraut. Thomas H. Raddall, "Happy Island," *Macleans*, November 1, 1946. — Tancook.

stinkplant — common name for a fish reduction plant, to which waste fishheads, defilleted backbones, and other fish

61

scrap are trucked to be converted into fishmeal for animal food. — Shelburne County.

stivver — stagger. — Cape Island. From E.M. Richardson's "From Norfolk to the Hawk."

stockkulp — stubborn. — Lunenburg.

stog — cram, pack, stuff, fill to the brim. — Marriott's Cove.

storm the kettle — boil water fast for a mugup (which see). — Lunenburg. See also **boil the kettle.**

storm-stayed — a common experience in the Maritimes, as in "the high school basketball team not only lost their game but were also storm-stayed in Halifax one night." — Shelburne *Coast Guard.* The Oxford English Dictionary lists this usage as Scottish.

stove in — "When the side of a boat is damaged so that it is pushed in or dented, they say it is *stove in.* This is an incorrect use of *stove* as the past tense of "stave," "to knock down, to push, to beat against." The word was commonly used in Scotland and northern England and at sea in British ships." — Ruth Lewis, "Why Did You Say That?" Rather than being incorrect, however, this form may simply be the preservation of the Middle English spoken form which survived because the scribes of the time were Norman French and had no interest in the spoken English language, imposing the more 'rational" French-based system of endings on Anglo-Saxon verbs ("stave," "staved").

straight as a loon's leg — metaphor to accompany "twisted as a ram's horn." — Barrington.

strange — state of mind causing one to exhibit fear or irrational behavior, as in the form, "When it come lobster season, I didn't get that far strange," (as to fear to go out on the boat). — Lunenburg. This use of the word is similar to the familiar Newfoundland warning to a stranger in the house, to make him relax, "Don't make strange!"

Lighthouse near Shelburne

strike — arrive. "When did you strike" — Barrington Passage.

struddle — upset things, fool with. "Don't struddle on the piano." — Lunenburg. From the German *strudeln*, "boil, spout, proceed rashly."

stulper — stumble. — Lunenburg. "You stulper over everything." From the German, *stolpern*, "to stumble."

suloo — silly person. — Lunenburg.

suttle — wash. — Lunenburg.

sweet humpbacked Jesus — West Middle Sable exclamation.

swonked — exhausted by labour. — Cape Sable Island. From E.M. Richardson's "From Norfolk to the Hawk,"*Dalhousie Review*, 1953.

tabernacle — footing for the mast, in the form of a square housing, on a small sailboat.

tallywagger — penis. "See that skipper over there? He has a 14-inch tallywagger!"

tedda-cakes — a local confection. — Chester.

tempest — thunder and lightning storm. — Little Harbour. "We wanted this rain, but we didn't want the tempest." — Clyde River. This use is also dialectal in England.

tended — nested in, frequented, habitually seen in vicinity. — Blanche. "Those ducks tended that pond over by Aubrey's." "That big duck's been tending around the back pasture." — Barrington.

tender — metaphorical use, by a body shop man looking under the rusty fender of an old van: "Yes, she's getting a little *tender* under there." — Cape Sable Island.

tending channel — keeping the log drive going down the river, in the channel of logs caught in the underbrush at the river's edge, by prying loose any big jams that result. — Barrington.

See also **making channel**.

they is one, they ain't one, they will be one by and bye, they is two,ect. — counting rhyme used to keep track of the number of rounds of yarn wound onto the **niddy-noddy** (which see).

have anything that's to think — "An aunt of mine used to say, meaning she couldn't think of anything more that she needed." — Lunenburg.

Tibb's Day, Tibb's Eve — the day after Resurrection, Judgement Day Eve. "I'll pay you Tibb's Day" — Chester. This expression must be very old, as the name "Tibb" occurs in the title of an early English Renaissance play, "John-John, Tib, His Wyf, and Sir John the Preest." C.L. Apperson, in *English Proverbs and Proverbial Phrases*, calls it a day "neither before nor after Christmas." Therefore, it is a euphemism for "never." The 1811 *Dictionary of the Vulgar Tongue* identifies it as Irish in origin. I suspect it to be an Elizabethan coinage, because of its irreverence about the Judgement Day.

tickle-y — having a fairly deep V bottom, said of a small boat: "That boat's maybe too tickle-y [or "tickle-ish"]; it's got quite a tickle onto it." — Barrington.

tiger sweat — lumbermen's homebrew. — Liverpool.

he's so tight, he'd skin a louse and tan the hide, and save the grease for tallow — an elaborate metaphorical way of saying that someone is miserly. — Barrington. "He was so mean he'd catch a louse and sell him for his hide and tallow." — Queens County.

Timberdoodle — local name for the woodcock. — Middle Clyde, Shelburne County.

tinker — undersized (by fishing regulations) lobster, mackerel. See also **jinker**.

tire — a cotton cover for a dress, worn by young girls to keep the dress clean. — Blanche. The Oxford English Dictionary lists this use as dating from 1425: "a pinafore or apron to protect a dress." Many examples occur in Shakespeare's plays and sonnets, with the word used to mean outer clothing of various kinds, including head-dresses, costumes, and coverlets: "If I had such a tire, this face of mine/ Were full as lovely as this of hers" (*Two Gentlemen of Verona*, IV, iv, 190-191); "Then put my tires and mantles on him whilst/ I wore his sword Philippan." (*Antony and Cleopatra,* II, v, 22-23).

tizick — consumption. — Shelburne.

tizicky — in fragile health, inclined to maladies of the chest. — Shelburne. "Brrrr, I'm cold, but then I'm tizicky."

toller — a duck-hunting dog, bred to look like a red fox, a small relative of the Golden Retriever, perhaps. It was developed in the nineteenth century in the Little River district of Yarmouth County; these dogs are still common in the area, and "little river duck-dogs" or "duck-toller" pups still fetch $100 in classified ads in local newspapers. The name "toller" comes from the dog's instinctual habit of "tolling" or calling ducks down to the shore of the ocean or lake, by playing around the edge like a red fox, so that the hunter may get a good shot at them. If properly trained, the toller will also dive into deep water and swim out to retrieve the duck. On Tancook Island, the word means "duck decoy," and is so identified as "middle English" by Thomas Raddall in "Happy Island," *Macleans*, November 1, 1946.

tomorrow next day — the indefinite future. — Lunenburg. See also **Tibb's Day**.

topdressing — euphemism for "manure." — Barrington.

t'other end — the name of a house, widely known in the area, at the end of the cove. — Chester.

t'other rooms — distinctive feature of a house with more than one room. See **off/on** and **father's t'other end**.

I'll tow that one alongside for a bit before I bring it aboard — an expression from Barrington Head to express doubt concerning the truth or believability of something someone just said.

town bicycle — the town prostitute, because "everybody rides her."

tracadie — "That's the tracadie," in Cape Sable Island, means "that's the way things have always been done."

turn the tea — pour the tea. — Cape Sable Island.

tutti frutti — lemon extract, consumed internally during prohibition days. — Upper Port Latour. See **cookie breath**.

twisted as a ram's horn — the opposite of "straight as a loon's leg." — West Green Harbour.

twitch — move logs down to the water from the woods, for the river log-drive. — Barrington.

twitch-road — crude logging trail along which logs are "twitched" down to the river for the log-drive. — Barrington.

ugly — cross, badtempered. — Barrington. The farmer warns the city dweller "Watch it, that dog's ugly." City dweller, not understanding, reaches to pet the dog, "Why no, that dog's *pretty*!"

upalong — "He's from upalong," means "he lives inland or up the shore." — Tancook Island.

Van Doos — Nova Scotia English pronunciation of the French name "Vingt-Deux" of the Royal 22nd Regiment, well-known Canadian fighting unit of the first World War.

vendor's — local name, in Lydgate, of a commercial bottled beer, not homebrew. "Yeah, gimme a vendor's!"

wants to — should, ought to. "A lot of men are building fiberglass hulls these days and finishing them themselves, thus saving a lot of money. They tell me these boats will last for years. The price they charge for them, they *want to*." — From "Coquewit Pass," *Paper Clip*, June 20, 1980. — Woods

Harbour. This use is listed by the Oxford English Dictionary as having originated in Northern England and the northern Midlands in England in 1563. It was regional in use in the Portland, Maine, area in the 1930s.

wackelass — "That cat is a regular wackelass," (it wiggles around underfoot). — Lunenburg. From the German *wackeln*, "to reel, totter," and *aas*, "carcass."

warping — moving a ship ahead by carrying the anchor out ahead by small boat, and dropping it, then winching the anchor rope aboard, thus hauling the ship forward. — Liverpool.

wed — old past tense form of "weed" — Blanche. "Yesterday I wed the garden." This word, from Old English *weod*, followed in spoken Middle English the analogy of Old English *creopan-creap*, "to creep."

wee waw — unsteady walk, zig-zag, wobble. — Cape Sable Island.

wet a line — go fishing. "That season I never wet a line." — Frank Parker Day's *Rockbound* (1945). — Lockeport.

wet moon/dry moon a sign of rain. A wet moon occurs when the horns of the crescent moon point upward, making the moon "hold water." The opposite, horns down, is a dry moon. — Cape Sable Island.

Whale-Birds — phalaropes. — Robie Tufts, *Birds of Nova Scotia*.

wharf rat — a ne-er do well, a person down and out. — Shelburne. This use was fairly common in Maine in the 1930s. The term may be compared with **rink rat** (which see in the *Concise Dictionary of Canadianisms*).

wheel — of a boat, the propeller, not the "helm" or steering wheel. — Upper Port Latour.
— a bicycle. — Baccaro.

wheelhouse — the cab of a pickup or truck. — Shelburne. A fisherman, hitch-hiking, started to jump into the back of the truck, and when invited to sit up front, said, "Good, I get to ride in the wheelhouse!"

where Bertram and Ira shot — a spot in the woods up the Roseway River, near Bear Den Hill, so named because two men, both Bowers, shot each other, each mistaking the other for a moose. — Ohio Road, Shelburne County.

whicker — horse's neigh. — Lunenburg. This term, unlike the many German-derived words in Lunenburg, occurs elsewhere mainly in England.

Whiskey-Jack — local name for the Gray Jay or Canada Jay. See also **Carryin'** Jay. — Lockeport.

Whistler — local name for the common golden-eye duck, perhaps because of "its fast-moving wings in flight," which make a "vibrant, sweet, whistling note." — Robie Tufts, *Birds of Nova Scotia*.

White-Wings — the willet. — Robie Tufts, *Birds of Nova Scotia*.

wind so sharp it cut the whiskers right off your face — Shelburne.

windlop — choppy surface of the sea when high wind ships it up. — Lunenburg.

window party — in which someone angry and probably drunk breaks windows, electronic equipment, etc., in someone's boat or house. — Upper Port Latour.

winkleaize — a three-cornered tear or rip. — Lunenburg. Compares with *winklehawk*, a name for the same thing from the Middle Atlantic (U.S.) linguistic survey.

with — "Are you coming with?" — Chester and Lunenburg. This is an exact imitation of a common German construction, "Kommen sie mit?"

woe-bawling — driving recklessly ("wobbling?") — Port Mouton.

woosh — bushy. — Lunenburg.

wootz — sound used to call a pig. — Lunenburg.

she certainly can put the work over the road — a compliment. — Smithville.

not worth two cents to jingle on a tombstone — worthless. — Barrington Head.

would — "You better would!" — Lunenburg.

wove — old past tense form of "wave." — Barrington. "They *wove* at us as they passed." This word, from Old English *wafian*, followed in spoken middle English the analogy of *shake-shook*.

yinkyank — local name for the dialect spoken by people from Southside, Cape Sable Island.

you — it is common to end nearly every sentence or phrase with "you", for emphasis, in Lockeport and other nearby areas. "I went to the store, you, and they were out of soap, you, so..." This use of the word suggests a similar rhythm and syntax in a construction found in Wales, England, where the rhythm word is "man": "Look you, man." In Sable River, nearby, the rhythm word is "yo."

A NOTE ON SOURCES

Most research in literature and language is done with printed texts. Folklore, however, is primarily oral; folklore research is based for the most part on language which is spoken and heard before the folklorist writes it down. My primary source, then, has been the people of the South Shore of Nova Scotia. Most of the items in this phrase book were used or heard by people I have met. Most of them were not young. Therefore, some phrases were more common in usage in the late 19th and early 20th century than they are now. However, the growing regional pride and the traditional high awareness of history and its legacy in the Maritimes have tended to keep old ways of speaking alive. In fact, much help came from historical societies, particularly in Shelburne and on Cape Sable Island, whose members I met at special meetings to discuss my project.

I wish to acknowledge also the special help given by two folklorists, Dr. Helen Creighton and Dr. Carmen Roy (of the National Museum of Man, Ottawa); by an anthropologist, Dr. Alyce Cheska (of the University of Illinois), who spends her summers at Sebim Beach and is doing research on recreation in the old days; and by Dr. Thomas H. Raddall, the novelist, of Liverpool, N.S.

I have made use of some printed sources as well. Many newspapers and periodicals of the area provided items, particularly the Shelburne *Coast Guard*, the *Paper Clip* from Ingomar, Shelburne's *Good Morning, Atlantic Insight*, and *Rural Delivery*, published in Port Joli. I am grateful to Ruth Lewis for the use of items from her article "Why Did You Say That?" in the *Nova Scotia Historical Quarterly* (Vol. 10, No. 3 & 4), December, 1980, p. 273. Evelyn M. Richardson's "From Norfolk to the Hawk" in the *Dalhousie Quarterly* (1953) provided not only several interesting phrases but also a provocative argument linking the language of Cape Sable Island and that of years ago in Cape Cod and Norfolk, England. I found several good items in an article on Tancook Island by Dr. Thomas H. Raddall published in *Macleans* November 1, 1946, and in several of his novels and stories. Several were either suggested in or corroborated in Helen Creighton's *Bluenose Magic* (1968), *Folklore of Lunenburg County* (1976), and *A Life in Folklore* (1975), all published by McGraw-Hill Ryerson. Robie Tufts kindly allowed me to include the local names of South Shore birds in his definitive *Birds of Nova Scotia* (Nova Scotia Museum). Finally, in doing research on the backgrounds of these words and phrases, I found the *Concise Dictionary of Canadianisms* (Gage, 1973), the *Oxford English Dictionary*, the American dialect survey worksheets, a range of dictionaries in several languages, and several proverb books, most useful. I am grateful to Professor Rex Wilson of the University of Western Ontario and to Professor Terrence Pratt of the University of Prince Edward Island, both experienced field linguists, who went over an early version of this manuscript and made valuable suggestions. Nevertheless, any mistakes are my own.

It will be of great help to me in this ongoing research project if readers who notice errors or additional items for inclusion will send them to me. I am also eager to make similar collections for other areas of Nova Scotia. I may be reached by mail at Upper Port Latour, N.S. B0W 3N0.